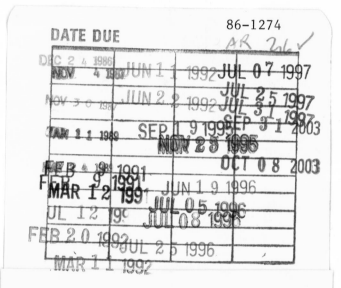

A New True Book

TREES

By Illa Podendorf

*This "true book" was prepared
under the direction of
Illa Podendorf,
formerly with the Laboratory School,
University of Chicago*

CHILDRENS PRESS, CHICAGO

Evergreens in winter

PHOTO CREDITS

Candee & Associates—2

Lynn M. Stone—4, 15, 17, 18 (bottom), 27 (bottom left), 35 (middle right, bottom right), 36 (top right and bottom)

James P. Rowan—6, 14 (left), 22, 33 (top right), 42, 44 (2 photos)

Kitty Kohout—8 (top), 13 (left), 27 (top left), 31, 32, 33 (top left & bottom left), 35 (top right, bottom left)

Reinhard Brucker—8 (bottom)

Julie O'Neil—13 (right)

M.M. Thoma—14 (right)

Bill Thomas—Cover, 18 (top), 21 (top), 29, 30, 36 (top left), 41

Jerry Hennen—21 (bottom), 27 (bottom right), 33 (bottom right), 34, 35 (top left)

James M. Mejuto—25 (top), 38 (2 photos)

Art Thoma—27 (top right)

M. Cole—25 (bottom)

Len W. Meents—10

Cover—Fall in Maine

Library of Congress Cataloging in Publication Data

Podendorf, Illa.
  Trees.

  (A New true book)
  Revised edition of: The true book of trees. 1954.
  Summary: Introduces the parts of a tree and
their functions, as well as the kinds of trees
and their place in the environment.
    1 Trees —Juvenile literature. [1. Trees]
I. Title.
QK475.8.P6   1982   582.16   81-12313
ISBN 0-516-01657-1   AACR2

86-1274

TABLE OF CONTENTS

Trees in a forest

PARTS OF A TREE

Trees are plants. They have the same parts as many other kinds of plants. Their trunks, limbs, and branches are their stems.

Live Oaks

Tree stems are made of wood. Food and water go up and down the stems. The stems hold leaves and twigs up to the sunshine.

Elm
flowers

Pine cones

The leaves make food
for the tree.

The cones or flowers
make seeds. New plants
grow from these seeds.

Roots gather food and
water from the soil. They
hold the tree firmly in the
ground.

RED OAK TREE

A tree has almost as many roots underground as there are branches above ground.

Different kinds of trees grow in different kinds of places.

Norway pine trees grow best where it is cold most of the time.

Palm trees grow where it is warm all year.

Palm trees in Hawaii

Norway Pine

13

Willow trees grow where there is a great deal of water.

Joshua trees grow where there is not much water.

Joshua tree

Weeping Willow

Sugar Maple leaves

HOW TREES GROW

All trees need water, air, and sunshine.

Tree leaves, like all green leaves, make their own food.

They make a kind of
sugar from water and air.
The heat of the sun
does the work.

Some of this food helps
a tree grow. Every year a
little is added to the ends
of the twigs and branches.

Some trees add a new
ring to their trunks each
year.

A tree keeps growing as
long as it lives.

White Oak

Dogwood
berries

18

Much of the food that
the leaves make is stored
in roots, stems, seeds, and
fruits.

The bark of a tree
protects the inside of the
tree from harm.

Some barks are smooth.
They grow as the tree
grows. Other barks do not
grow as fast as the tree.
These barks are cracked
and not smooth.

Sometimes trees lose
some of their bark. A living
tree will always grow a
new bark.

White Birch
bark

Ponderosa Pine
bark

21

Rocky Mountain National Park, Long's Peak in background

TWO GROUPS OF TREES

Some trees have needles or scalelike leaves. These are called evergreens.

Most of these trees have cones. They lose their needles or leaves a few at a time.

Some trees have broad leaves.

Broadleaf trees have flowers quite different from cones. Some tree flowers are beautiful.

Most of these trees lose all of their leaves in the fall. They get new ones in the spring.

Every tree belongs to one of these two groups.

Top: Although this wisteria looks like a tree, it is really a woody vine.
Left: Flowering crab

NEEDLELEAF TREES

White pines have five needles in a bundle.

Red pines have two needles together.

Spruce needles are four-sided.

Cedar trees have folded scales instead of needles.

Balsam fir trees have soft, flat needles.

Common juniper trees have very sharp, pointed needles.

Red Cedar

Juniper

Spruce

White Pine

These are some
evergreen trees.

27

Sequoias are big trees. They are the biggest of all trees.

Some of them were old trees when America was discovered.

Sequoias have cones.

General Sherman, a giant Sequoia

Redwood forest

Redwoods are big trees, too.
Redwoods have cones.

American Holly

BROADLEAF TREES

Holly trees are broadleaf trees.

Shade trees have many branches. They have many leaves.

Maple and elm trees are good shade trees.

All kinds of ash trees make good shade trees.

Birch trees are shade trees, too.

Cottonwood leaves are noisy in the wind. This is because the leaves have flat stems.

Cottonwood

Top left: Green Ash
Top right: Cottonwood tree
Left: American, or White, Elm
Above: Sugar Maple

33

Ohio Buckeye

LEAF PARTS AND SHAPES

Some leaves have many parts.

The parts are called leaflets.

You can know the name of a tree by knowing the shape of its leaves.

Above: American Holly

Above: Aspen leaves
Below: White Elm leaves

Above: White Oak leaves
Below: Sugar Maple

Above: Collecting
maple syrup
Above right:
Orange tree
Right: Red-headed
Woodpecker

USES OF TREES

Trees give us fruits.
Trees give us nuts.
Trees give us turpentine.
Trees give us maple
syrup.

Without trees, many
animals and birds would
have no homes.

Houses are made of wood.

Paper is made from wood, too.

People use wood in their homes, too.

Wood is used to make many things. How many things can you think of that are made from wood?

A woods of broadleaf trees is beautiful in fall when the leaves change color.

Leaves do not need frost to change color. They will change without frost.

Sassafras trees

Fall in the Porcupine Mountains

PROTECT TREES

Trees give beauty to our land.

Trees give us many things we use every day.

Trees help keep the soil from washing away.

Apple Orchard

Evergreens in Glacier National Park

Protect the trees—their trunks and branches, leaves and roots—so they can live and grow.

Work to make sure new trees are planted as old ones are cut.

Trees are an important and beautiful part of our world.

WORDS YOU SHOULD KNOW

balsam (BALL•sum) — a type of evergreen tree with short needles

bark — a tough outside part of a woody plant

broad (BRAWD) — wide; big from side to side

branch — the part of tree that grows out from the trunk

cone (KOHN) — the part of an evergreen tree that has the seeds

elm (ELM) — a tall broadleaf tree with pointy-edged leaves

firm (FERM) — solid; not loose

frost (FRAWST) — a covering of thin ice

Joshua (JOSH•oo•wah) — a type of tree that grows in the deserts of the United States

juniper (JOO•nih•per) — a type of evergreen tree with small needles and blue berries

limb (LIM) — a large branch of a tree

maple (MAY•pul) — a broadleaf tree that grows all over the northern half of the world and that makes winged fruit seeds

palm (PAHM) — a type of tree that grows in warm parts of the world

protect (proh•TEKT) — keep safe

root — the part of a plant that grows down into the ground

scalelike (SKAIL•lyk) — to look like the skin of fish; to be made of small, thin, overlapping parts

sequoia (sih•KWOY•ah) — a type of evergreen tree with short needles that can reach a height of over 300 feet

spruce (SPROOS) — a type of evergreen tree with short needles

stem — the part of a tree that keeps it up

trunk — the tall main stem of a tree

turpentine (TER•pen•tyn) — a thin oil made from parts of some evergreen trees

twig — a small tree branch

willow (WILL•oh) — a type of tree with thin twigs and narrow leaves

woods — a place where many trees grow close together; forest

INDEX

About the Author

*Born and raised in western Iowa, Illa Podendorf has had experience teaching
science at both elementary and high school levels. For many years she served
as head of Science Department, Laboratory School, University of Chicago and
is currently consultant on the series of True Books and author of many of them.
A pioneer in creative teaching, she has been especially successful in working
with the gifted child.*